Divinely Ordinary
Divinely Human

Divinely Ordinary
Divinely Human

Celebrating
the
Life and Work
of
Eileen Caddy

Compiled and edited by David Earl Platts

FINDHORN
Press

First published in 1999

ISBN 1-899171-87-8

British Library Cataloguing-in-Publication Data.
A catalogue record for this book is available from the British Library.

Library of Congress Catalog Card Number: 99-64802

Photograph of Findhorn Village, page 54, © 1999 Kathleen Thormod Carr
Jacket photograph © Corbis Images 1999
Layout and design by Pam Bochel
Jacket design by Thierry Bogliolo

Printed and bound by WSOY, Finland

Published by
Findhorn Press

The Park, Findhorn
Forres IV36 3TY
Scotland, UK
Tel 01309 690582
Fax 01309 690036

P.O. Box 13939
Tallahassee
Florida 32317-3939, USA
Tel 850 893 2920
Fax 850 893 3442

e-mail info@findhornpress.com
findhornpress.com

ACKNOWLEDGMENTS

Several people have taken part in creating this book. I am deeply grateful to:

- Thierry and Karin Bogliolo for giving me the opportunity to compile and edit it

- Carol Shaw for ferreting out many of the photographs

- Brian Crawford Young and the Findhorn Foundation Visuals Department for their assistance

- The photographers for the use of their pictures

- Roy McVicar for editing the first six books of Eileen Caddy's guidance

- Pam Bochel for her patience, skill and magic in transforming a collection of words and images into a beautiful book

- Lorna Richardson for her suggestions and support

- Eileen Caddy for her guidance, inspiration and friendship

David Earl Platts
Knaphill, England

FOREWORD

While I was talking to a group of young people, the subject of the Findhorn Foundation came up. After listening to some of my experiences of the early days when it was just coming into being, and of the wonderful spirit of creativity, adventure and enthusiasm that existed then, one of the women exclaimed wistfully, "Where is the Findhorn for our generation? Where is the place where we can pioneer a new spirit?"

However ancient the community may seem to those who weren't even born in the early seventies when Peter and Eileen Caddy, Dorothy Maclean, and I were its co-directors, it is still a place of pioneering spirit and spiritual potential, capable of being every bit as exciting and wondrous now as it was for us then. However the question is actually misdirected. For it was not the place that was so wonderful and alive with possibility, but the people who inhabited it.

Findhorn became famous because of the amazing vegetables that grew in its nutrient-deficient soil, but the community itself grew from the spirit of all those who lived there. And of those people, it is safe to say that Findhorn would not exist had it not been for Eileen Caddy.

Of course, Peter and Dorothy, the other two original founders, contributed invaluable and unique gifts without which Findhorn would not have come into being. But Eileen was the voice of God in the community, the axis around which the whole revolved. For in the final analysis, what made – and makes – Findhorn powerful as a spiritual centre is not its garden or its work with nature spirits or its educational programmes, but its focus on discovering and aligning with the God within, the sacredness within each of us and within all things. It was the ability to be quiet and listen to the 'still small voice within' that created Findhorn and that was the greatest and purest lesson and gift it had to offer those who came there. The miracles of vegetation and manifestation were truly wondrous, but in the end, it is the source of the miracles that is most important.

Eileen Caddy embodies why the community came into being in the first place: to be a sign in our modern age when spirit often seems so far removed as to be simply a fantasy, that God is present in each of us – an accessible source of belonging, connection and miracles.

I have had the privilege of knowing Eileen in many of the ordinary ways that fill our lives. I have seen her serving tea and cookies, hanging out laundry, cleaning the kitchen, being a mom. I have seen her courage in meeting ill health, the death of friends, the challenges of relationship, the ending of a marriage. I have seen her angry, sad, happy, supportive and questioning. And in the midst of all the ordinary feelings and thoughts that belong to a person who lives a rich, challenging and productive life, I have seen one consistent truth about her: she is the one who listens.

She listens because she knows, with a hard-won, life-tempered shining steel of a knowing, that God speaks to her, all the time, each moment, just as God speaks to you and to me and to each life and seed and atom in creation. And that still small voice speaks not just in words, but in a language of love and empowerment, caring and embracing, oneness and co-creativity.

The God within is no stranger to her but a real presence in the midst of joys and sorrows, possibilities and challenges. Because it is real to her, she has a gift of making it real to others. For her, 'unconditional love' is no catchy new-age slogan but a real force that is the fundamental language in which this presence speaks. And when you are with Eileen, you can feel her encouraging and supporting you to listen too, deeper perhaps than you have ever listened before, to hear that language in your own heart and mind and be transformed by it.

I look upon Eileen as one of the premier mystics of our time, and as a wonderfully ordinary woman who has demonstrated over and over again the power that lies in our ordinariness. She brings God down to earth for us, and she can bring us down to earth as well, down into the fabric of our lives wherein the still small voice speaks and works its magic.

Eileen Caddy has shown us what can emerge from the life of one who listens. She has done so with grace, with courage, with humor and with undaunted love. To know Eileen is to know that we too can be among those who listen and hear.

"Where is the Findhorn for our generation?" my young friend asked. The real question is where are those in our generation who can listen deeply to the voice of the sacred in all its many forms and longings, who can hear the still small voice and its language of unconditional love?

It is those who, like Eileen, will build not just new Findhorns, but more importantly, a new world for our future. And if they live as passionately, lovingly and clearly with that inner voice as Eileen has, it will be a good world indeed.

David Spangler
March 1999

EDITOR'S NOTE

This book is a tribute to an ordinary woman

who has lived an extraordinary life.

It presents selected highlights of her life and work,

a full account of which may be found in her autobiography,

Flight Into Freedom.

EARLY CHILDHOOD IN EGYPT

Eileen Marion Jessop was born on August 26, 1917, in Alexandria, Egypt, where her father had moved from Ireland to work in the Anglo-Egyptian Bank, and where later he had met her English mother. Eileen was the second of four children, with an older brother Patrick (Paddy), a younger brother, Rex, and sister, Florence (Torrie).

Eileen's father, Albert William Jessop

Eileen's mother, Muriel Clutten (Bull) Jessop

Just old enough to sit up and smile for the photographer

With her mother in a horse-drawn carriage

A young sailor, aged three, standing at attention and giving a proper salute

In costume as a fairy, aged four, with Torrie, and Rex and Paddy dressed as chefs for a fancy dress party

SCHOOL DAYS IN IRELAND

When she was six, Eileen and Paddy were sent off to school in Ireland where they lived with an aunt in Dublin during the school year. Rex and Torrie later joined them as they became of school age. Her aunt awakened in Eileen a deep longing to know more about God.

Eileen, aged seven, in Fernhurst, Dublin

She loved her dolls, especially Nanouche

With Paddy

Clockwise from top left:
• With Paddy and her aunt; • on her way
to feed the ducks at Stephens Green;
• feeding the animals at Dublin Zoo;
• playing cricket with her brothers; • fishing
in the river with her sister; • resting after
playing tennis.

ADOLESCENCE

Eileen lived with her aunt until she was eleven years old when she and Torrie were sent to a succession of boarding schools. Every summer the children visited their parents in Alexandria. Eileen had the responsibility of looking after Paddy, Rex and Torrie on the five-day train and boat journey between Ireland and Egypt.

Sailing on board the *Esperia* en route to Egypt for the school holidays

Celebrating her 16th birthday in Egypt
Clockwise from bottom right: Eileen, her mother, Torrie, a servant and Rex

Rex, Eileen and Torrie at the beach in 1934

A family outing down by the beach with Torrie, her mother, Rex and Eileen

Torrie and Eileen as bridesmaids at a wedding in Egypt
From the left: Torrie, her aunt, her mother and Eileen

When her father died unexpectedly of peritonitis, Eileen left school to return to Egypt to look after her mother and Rex who suffered from epilepsy. Eventually her mother decided they would all move to England. However, within a year of moving she became ill with meningitis and died suddenly. The children had lost both their parents in less than two years. Eileen was only 18.

With her brothers in England

Sunning and sewing in an English garden

During the next three years Eileen went to a domestic science college in Sussex, worked as a cook in a school in the New Forest, and at Paddy's suggestion, used their inheritance to buy and run a public house with him.

Her wedding day,
complete with a
Guard of Honour

MARRIAGE AND FAMILY

The public house was near a Royal Air Force (RAF) base in Oxfordshire, and soon Eileen met a tall, good-looking officer. Andrew Combe was a squadron leader and one of three pilots who were the first to fly single-engine bombers non-stop from Egypt to Darwin, Australia – a record flight in 1939. Andrew and Eileen were married in May of that year.

Eileen Marion Jessop.

With

Squadron Leader and Mrs. Andrew R. Combe's

Compliments.

Starbarrow,
Church Avenue,
Farnborough, Hants.   13th May, 1939.

Small animals,
such as Toby,
a miniature Griffon,
have always been favourites

The war began, and as with most Forces families, they were moved regularly every three years, first from Farnborough where Jennifer and Richard were born, to Norfolk where Suzanne was born, and then to London where they survived the ravages of the Blitz. After the war they were posted to the United States where Mary Elizabeth was born. Then it was back to England. They bought a large house for their growing family in Surrey, and had their last child, Penny. Subsequently they were posted to Habbanya, Iraq.

Eileen with four of her children, Mary Elizabeth, Jennifer, Richard and Suzanne, in 1949

With her youngest daughter, Penny, by the swimming pool in Iraq

THE DIVINITY WITHIN

After fourteen years of marriage, and back in England again, Eileen unexpectedly fell in love with Peter Caddy, an RAF officer she and Andrew had known for quite some time. She asked Andrew for a divorce, thinking that, given enough time to work it out, they could end their marriage amicably. She became most distressed when Andrew, and later a court order, forbade her from seeing her children. Bewildered by the chain of events, Eileen went into a Glastonbury sanctuary with Peter and his ex-wife, Sheena, and began to pray.

I was feeling greatly troubled, and I was asking God what I should do because everything in my life seemed in such a hopeless state. I was right in the middle of my very serious talk when suddenly I heard very clearly a voice talking to me. The voice said, 'Be still and know that I am God'. I opened my eyes and looked around to find who had spoken to me. Even though Peter and Sheena were in the sanctuary, I could see neither of them was talking to me. They were both deep in prayer themselves, with their eyes shut. The voice was inside my head.

After a moment, I heard the same voice again. It went on to say, 'You have taken a very big step in your life. But if you follow My voice all will be well. I have brought you and Peter together for a very special purpose, to do a specific work for Me. You will work as one, and you will realise it more fully as time goes on. There are few who have been brought together in this way. Don't be afraid, for I am with you'.

Later, when I had finished in the sanctuary, I went outside. I told Peter and Sheena exactly what had happened and what I had heard. They both became very excited and made me repeat what I had heard. As I repeated it, I realised what special words they are, 'Be still, and know that I am God'.

I had always thought of God as someone who was 'out there', someone I could talk to, but who never seemed to answer me in actual words. Yet here I was hearing a voice that said it was the voice of God. What did it all mean?

I found after that first experience of hearing the voice every time I sat quietly by myself, the voice would talk to me. I discovered that when I asked it questions, it would give me the answers. I soon learned that here was a wonderful friend who was present when I needed help. I could talk to my friend at any time, and I would always get an answer.

As time went on, and I got used to the voice, I found myself doing whatever it asked me to do. I began to accept that it must be a very wise voice. My faith in it became stronger and stronger, and I found myself turning to the voice to guide me in all I was doing.

In the beginning, the voice called me 'My child', and it was just like a very loving parent talking to its child. Then somehow our relationship changed, and the voice began to call me, 'My beloved child', and my love for the voice grew deeper and deeper. When you are called a beloved child, it gives you a lovely warm, special feeling inside.

Then the time came when the voice called me, 'My beloved', and I began to feel that this wonderful voice was right here within my own being, within my own heart, and my love for it grew even deeper. I could feel a oneness with it, as if nothing could ever separate me from it, that it was always here as part of me, morning, noon and night. It did not matter what I was doing or where I was, that voice was right here.

Now, after listening to the voice for more than 46 years, I have come to accept it as an expression of the highest part of myself, the divinity within me.

It is her guidance from within which she has lived by ever since first hearing the voice in 1953, and which has inspired the creation and early development of the Findhorn Foundation, the international spiritual community and holistic education centre in northern Scotland. Messages Eileen has received from her inner voice appear throughout the remainder of this book.

NEW BEGINNINGS

Eileen became pregnant, and a son, Christopher, was born in London. Peter resigned from the RAF and took a job at the Air University in Hampshire where Jonathan was born. Later they moved to Scotland, and eventually settled in Forres. Peter was employed as manager of the Cluny Hill Hotel, and it was there they had their last child, David.

High Street of the Royal Burgh of Forres
with monument and clock tower

The Cluny Hill Hotel, Forres

With Peter, Jonathan and Christopher in the Cluny Hill Hotel garden overlooking the municipal golf course

❦ I Am Within You ❦

I am with you whether you ascend to the heights or sink to the depths. I am there.
I am with you in the silence when all is peace and harmony. Yet I am there when you
call upon Me when you are in trouble, and all is chaos and confusion around you.
I am closer than breathing, nearer than hands and feet. I am within you, within all creation.

It is not necessary to wear sackcloth and ashes or to go around declaring that
you are a miserable sinner and are not worthy to be called My beloved child.
All this teaching is false and unreal. Accept that we are one and that I am within you.

Remember, always let your faith and confidence be in Me, the divinity within you.
Walk hand in hand with Me; consult Me at all times; and let Me guide and direct you.
I am within you, therefore nothing from without can interfere with our direct contact.
Feel safe and secure in this knowledge.

❦

I am within you. Accept with joy and wonderment our oneness.
Accept it as a very small child, and do not waste time and energy trying to work it out
with your mind. If you try to approach this life intellectually, you waste much time and fail
to see the simplicity of it. My ways are simple; cease making them complicated for yourself.

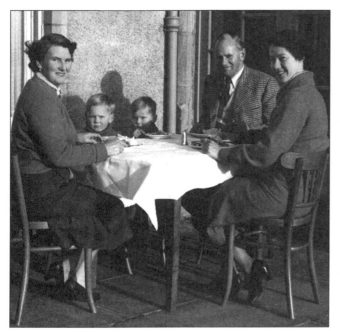

Lunching outside the Cluny Hill Hotel with Peter and Dorothy Maclean, a Canadian friend employed as Peter's secretary

David, Christopher and Jonathan

The Caddy family, 1960

❧ Play ❧

Live and work, but do not forget to play, to have fun in life and enjoy it.
You need balance in everything. Too much work and no play makes life lopsided,
and makes you dull and uninteresting. Seek perfect balance in everything you do,
and you will find life a real joy.
You need variety in life, so why not break out and attempt something quite new
and different, not because you are bored with what you are doing or
because you want to run away from it, but because you realise you need a change?
When you can do it without any sense of guilt, you will find you will be able
to do all you have to do with a new outlook;
and, what is more, you will be able to do it with real enjoyment.
What is the use of life unless you can enjoy it and have a good time
in everything you undertake, whether you call it work or play?

Life should never be a burden.
You are not here to be bowed down by the weight of the world.
You are here to make the very most of life and enjoy every moment of it
because you are living a balanced life, and there is a constant giving and receiving.

Right: Cruising on nearby Findhorn Bay
with Peter and the children

❧ The Present ❧

Rejoice and give eternal thanks, for you know that you live forever.
You do it one day at a time, living each moment fully and gloriously, forgetting the past,
with no concern for the future, simply accepting that life is eternal
and has no beginning and no end.

Ponder on the words 'Now is the time'. See the secret of a joyous, harmonious,
satisfying life, as you accept that now is the only time. Now is the only time there is.
No longer dwell on the past, nor look for some future good.
Awake to the glorious now which is filled with all the goodness of God. Accept it all.
Accept the truth that understanding is yours now. Healing is yours now.
Abundant limitless supply is yours now. Harmony is yours now. Protection is yours now.
Peace is yours now. Joy is yours now.

Never try to look too far ahead; that in itself can cause great strain and distress.
You can only take one step at a time, so take that one step,
and the next will follow at exactly the right time.
Let things unfold, and do not try to manipulate them.

FINDHORN BAY CARAVAN PARK

Peter and Eileen worked very closely together in managing the hotel. He would ask her to get inner guidance on how to resolve problems as they arose, and then he would implement it. They were very successful, and during their tenure the Cluny Hill Hotel was upgraded to four-star status. After five years they were transferred to a hotel in Perthshire; however they were discharged abruptly without explanation at the end of their first season there.

Having nowhere to live, they moved their small caravan to an isolated corner of the Findhorn Bay Caravan Park on the Moray Firth where they spent the winter. The following spring they added an annex for Dorothy Maclean and an enclosed patio, and as Peter was still unemployed and receiving National Assistance, they started a vegetable garden.

Their caravan and Lagonda car

Dorothy found she had a special resonance with plants, and she began to receive inner messages from the spiritual forces behind nature which she called 'devas'. The group carefully followed the messages which often described specific needs of the vegetables they were growing, and despite the harsh climate of northeast Scotland and the poor soil, their garden flourished.

Their spiritual practice was a very important part of each day. Every morning and evening the three adults meditated and did other inner work together. They continued their practice, started while at the Cluny Hill Hotel, to radiate out blessings to a list of people and to various centres around the world. Eileen was assured from within that she and her first family would be reconciled one day. She was told to keep her heart open and the love flowing to them; and so she radiated love every day to each of her first five children and to Andrew, and affirmed their reconciliation. In addition she meditated several hours each evening by herself and kept a written record of all guidance she received.

Dorothy, Eileen and Peter on the patio, with their garden nestling in the sand dunes beyond

❧ *Lessons* ❧

*You may not always understand why you find yourself where you are, but you may be sure
there is a very good reason, and there is a lesson to be learned. Do not fight against it,
but find out what that lesson is and learn it quickly so you can move on and grow.*

*Never fail to give thanks for every lesson you learn, no matter how difficult it may be.
Realise that only the very best is bound to come out of it, and that every difficulty is but a
stepping stone along the way. There are important lessons which have to be learned,
and the sooner you learn them, the better.*

*If you have made a mistake, admit it, say you are sorry and move on.
Then no precious time is wasted in trying to justify yourself and prove you are right.
You have many lessons to learn.
Learn them quickly, and try never to make the same mistake twice.*

*When you refuse to learn a lesson one way, it will be presented to you in another way.
There is always the easy way, but when you refuse to accept it, the more difficult
way will be presented to you. Why not learn your lessons the easy way!
Life is very simple. Why make it difficult for yourself?*

THE BIRTH OF COMMUNITY

For three years they lived a relatively secluded life, and then Eileen received the guidance, "A whole new world is opening up for you. Be not afraid. This centre is becoming a beacon of light which will draw souls to it. Turn no one away." Their first visitors arrived in 1965. Two years later booklets of Eileen's guidance were prepared and distributed to people asking for them, and as news spread of the group co-creating with the spiritual forces behind nature, more and more people came to see for themselves the marvellous garden growing virtually on a beach.

In time people asked to join with them, and during the next few years bungalows as well as caravans were added to the site. As the numbers of people increased and a sense of community grew, a central kitchen and dining room were built, followed by a sanctuary and craft studios. People gathered in the sanctuary before work each morning to meditate and to hear Peter read out the guidance Eileen had received the previous evening. In 1971 she was instructed from within to stop sharing her guidance with the others as the time had come for them to make deliberate contact with their own inner divinity and to receive their own inner direction.

Cedarwood bungalows around the central garden

Clockwise from top left: Eileen, Peter, Dorothy, Christopher, David and Jonathan

Community kitchen and dining room under construction

Moving Forward

You must be prepared for wonderful changes to take place.
If you can accept them and simply absorb them like a piece of blotting paper,
the changes will come about within and around you in great peace and harmony.
You will find that you will change with the changes without being unduly affected by them
and that you will live and move and breathe in them as naturally as a fish does in water.
You will be able to accept your new environment and
become perfectly adjusted to it without any strain.
A child moves from kindergarten to primary and from primary to secondary school
without any difficulty because it takes it all in its stride and moves forward step by step,
accepting each new subject and adjustment as it comes. It could not be moved
straight from kindergarten to secondary, for it would be completely lost.
Do not be concerned; I will not move you too swiftly. All is in My perfect timing.

Flow with the tide, and not against it. When you feel that change is necessary,
be willing to change and change quickly, and do not try to resist it.

It is amazing how soon you can get used to change as long as you have the courage
and conviction that the changes which are taking place are all for the very best.

Preparing a meal for the growing
community with Vance Martin

The dining room was also used
as a gathering place for
meetings, musical sharings
and fun nights

Nothing is by Chance

*Nothing is by chance. There is a perfect pattern and plan running through the whole of life,
and you are part of that wholeness, therefore part of that perfect pattern and plan.
When you see strange things happening in your life, and wonder why they happen to you,
take time to look for that perfect pattern and plan, and see how it all fits in,
and you will see a reason for everything.*

*Never waste time and energy wishing you were somewhere else, doing something else.
Accept your situation and realise you are where you are,
doing what you are doing, for a very specific reason.
Realise that nothing is by chance, that you have certain lessons to learn,
and that the situation you are in has been given to you to enable you to learn those lessons
as quickly as possible, so that you can move onward and upward along this spiritual path.*

*Experiences, no matter how strange or difficult, have been given to you for a purpose;
therefore take the time to look for that purpose. Try to see My hand in everything,
to see that nothing is by chance, and that there is no such thing as luck or good fortune.
Realise that you draw to yourself all the very best or the very worst in life.*

Outside the
Park
sanctuary

❧ *Kingdom of Heaven* ❧

Know that the kingdom of heaven is within you; it is there waiting for you to recognise it.
You must know it, believe it and then bring it about.
The kingdom of heaven is a state of mind, and it is for everyone to seek and find.

❧

A seed has to be planted in the soil before it can grow.
It has within it all its potential, but that potential remains dormant
until given the right conditions in which to grow and develop.
You have within you the kingdom of heaven, but unless you wake up to the fact
and start searching for it, you will not find it, and there it will remain.
There are many souls in this life who will not wake up to this fact,
and they are like seeds stored away in packets.

❧

I am spirit. I am everywhere. I am in everything and everyone.
There is nowhere where I am not.
When you fully realise it, and can accept it, you know that the kingdom of heaven
is within you; you can cease your search and turn within.
Then you find within you all you are looking for. Life is no longer complicated
but becomes simplicity itself. It simply means that you have to stop and take time to be still
and to seek within for everything, and there you will find it.

Guidance on the Park sanctuary door

Interior of the Park sanctuary

Alone in prayer in the Park sanctuary

FAITH AND PRAYER

Once I was reading the Bible and I read a passage which I had read many times, but this time the words seemed to stand out for me, and I wondered what they meant. These were the words of Jesus, "If you have faith as a grain of mustard seed, you will say to this mountain, 'Move from here to there', and it will move; and nothing will be impossible to you." (Matthew 17:20, Revised Standard Version)

As I thought about these words and meditated upon them, I wondered what could be the highest and seemingly most insurmountable mountain standing in front of humanity right now, one which needs to be removed through 'faith as a grain of mustard seed'. The mountain which came to me was 'fear'. I feel there is so much fear in the world that it is like a canker, eating away all of the good, the positive, the beautiful, and leaving all of the negative and rotten. It is strangling humanity.

Fear is one of our greatest enemies. I know it can hold me back from doing what I need to do. But I realise that unless I am willing to face my fears, I can never get rid of them. I have found that as long as I try to avoid my fears, they can become like monsters, and when I have the courage to confront them, they begin to become more manageable, and sometimes even fade away into nothingness.

The way I deal with my fears is with faith and prayer. Faith is greater and more powerful than fear. I affirm my faith and trust that all is well with the world, that a vast plan is unfolding, that all is in the hands of the Creator and that whatever is happening in my life is for the very best.

How do I pray? To set the pace for the day, I have a time of attunement in the early morning on awakening, before my mind can become embroiled in all the events and activities of the day. I find my life then is like a clean canvas without a mark on it. For me, these first strokes upon waking need to be very clear and definite, full of love, inspiration and expectancy for the new day ahead.

I tap into the highest level of my being, the divinity within, and communicate with it. I have faith that all my needs are being wonderfully met, even before I communicate them. This is where faith in my contact with the divinity within is so necessary. When I start the day off in this way, I know the day will be full of wonders because I am living in harmony with divine laws.

❧

First thing every morning, I say, 'Here I am God, use me in any way'. I offer myself to be used in any way, realising I have to take the consequences when I do. Then I spend time in prayer and meditation, having first read the piece for the day in Opening Doors Within. *I do it in my bedroom before going to the sanctuary to meditate further. I feel that what I am doing in the sanctuary is anchoring the Christ energies for the whole community. I am there to centre, balance and stabilise myself, and to go on into my everyday life and live it.*

One day I was saying, 'Thy will be done' and as I said it I realised that I was separating myself from God – there was God and there was Eileen, and somehow or other there was something wrong with this separation. I had had guidance over and over again that 'We are one, there is no separation', but I didn't realise it in my heart. I felt awful about it, and at the same time felt that if I did believe it in my heart I would be a heretic. Very gradually, however, I grew to feel that God is within and that has become a deep inner knowing. It has become alive within me. I know with all my being that, yes, God and I are one. There is no separation. God is within.

It has been a process. It didn't just happen straight away. I have had to work with it, be with it, live with it and embody it until I have come to know that, yes, I am the guidance. What comes through me is from the very highest part of my being, the divinity within.

❧

THE FINDHORN FOUNDATION

The 1970s were a decade of rapid growth. Eileen's first book of guidance, *God Spoke To Me,* was published in 1971. Then the British Broadcasting Corporation (BBC) presented a live television programme from the caravan park, featuring the nationally known and respected broadcaster, Magnus Magnusson. Newspaper articles and books also began to appear. An American journalist, Paul Hawken, wrote *The Magic of Findhorn,* and the community, now officially a charitable trust called the Findhorn Foundation, published *The Findhorn Garden.*

The Foundation continued to expand, and began to attract more and more people from beyond the United Kingdom. The American writer, educator and mystic, David Spangler, became co-director with Peter, and he with his partner, Myrtle Glines, contributed significantly to the early development of the Foundation. By 1975 it had grown to 350 people.

David Spangler,
Myrtle Glines,
Peter and Eileen
at Randolph's Leap,
a nature setting on
the Findhorn River
near Forres

✿≈ God's Community ≈✿

The work of this centre is to: raise the vibrations by the awareness of the
Christ consciousness within each one; find direct contact with Me;
create light and more light and radiate it out; bring down My kingdom on earth
and see it start right here and go out and out to the four corners of the earth;
know with that inner knowing all things are possible
and see the impossible become possible;
create wholeness and oneness; and bring unity in diversity.

I want you to see this centre of light as an ever-growing cell of light.
It started as a family group; it is now a community; it will grow into a village,
then into a town and finally into a vast city of light.
It will progress in stages and expand very rapidly. Expand with the expansion.
The foundations go very very deep and are built on rock;
therefore it now does not matter how fast the growth takes place.
It does not matter how great it grows.

*See this centre in its true perfection,
filled with souls who are here
simply to do My will and
walk in My ways.*

And Eileen's Findhorn family
grew and grew

When the Foundation needed additional accommodation to house the incoming waves of people, it purchased the Cluny Hill Hotel, which as Cluny Hill College, became the centre of its educational programmes and conferences. Later, other properties were acquired including Station House in the village of Findhorn and Drumduan in Forres. The Foundation also accepted custodianship of Traigh Bhan, a retreat house on the island of Iona, as well as the entire island of Erraid off the west coast of Scotland. In her meditations Eileen linked the properties together as parts of the whole, and radiated love and light to them each day.

Cluny Hill College, the Findhorn Foundation's education centre, in winter

❧ *Patience* ❧

When a small child learning to walk falls down, it is not discouraged, but picks itself up
and tries again and again until it has mastered the art of walking. So with the spiritual life.
Never at any time allow seeming defeats to discourage you from advancing
along the spiritual path. If you fall, simply pick yourself up and try again.
Be not content to lie there in self-pity and say you cannot carry on
and that life is too difficult. Your attitude must always be that of absolute inner certainty
that once your feet have been set upon the spiritual path, you will reach the goal in the end,
no matter what obstacles you may meet along the way.
You will find time spent alone in the silence recharges you spiritually
and helps you to face whatever is ahead without flinching or faltering.
That is why time spent alone with Me each morning
helps to fortify you for whatever the day may bring.

Be silent and your heart will sing with joy.
See no separation and you will find oneness.
Be gentle and you will need no power.
Be patient and you will achieve all things.

Grand opening of
the sauna at
Station House in
Findhorn village

The village
of Findhorn
on the
Moray Firth

❧ The Whole ❧

It takes all sorts to make up the whole. Every tiny screw, cog and spring is needed
to make a clock. Every organ of the body, every tiny cell and atom, is needed
to make up the whole perfect body. When you see yourself as part of the whole
you will no longer want to withhold what you have to give.

Let there be no feeling of competition within you.
When you realise everyone has a specific part to offer to the whole,
all that spirit of competition will disappear, and you will be able to relax and be yourself.

Use all you have for the benefit of the whole. Do not try to accumulate or hoard it,
but share it; for as you share, so will it grow; whereas if you try to hold on
and possess something or someone, you will surely lose it.
It is the law, and as you live it, you will see it working out all around you.

When all souls give of their very best, the weight and responsibility do not fall
on the shoulders of the few. The burden is lightened for the whole,
until it is no longer a burden but a real joy and pleasure.
Watch your attitude, and contribute to the joy and smooth running of the whole.

Stone cottages on the island of Erraid looking across to the island of Mull

With a group of islanders talking to a goat

Dressed for dinner

Peter and Eileen Caddy, Joan Hartnell-Beavis, ROC (Robert Ogilvie Crombie) and Dorothy Maclean

With her sons from both marriages together for the first time, Christopher, David, Richard and Jonathan

Above: By the original caravan with Dorothy Maclean

In the Universal Hall for a Friday night 'Sharing' with Peter

With her sister, Torrie, and brother, Paddy, on Eileen's 70th birthday

Meditating while visiting a friend in Montreal

Right: On tour in the USA

With David Earl Platts signing their books at the Phoenix Shop in the caravan park

Celebrating her birthday with Findhorn Press publishers Karin and Thierry Bogliolo and co-author David Earl Platts

By the front door of her home

Right: Tea time with Crystal

Having a bird to tea on the patio

Blessing the land for a new home to be built

Resting on a bench presented to her by Greuthof, a German publisher of her books, to commemorate her 80th birthday

All her eight children together for the first time to celebrate Eileen's 80th birthday in 1997

When her family had grown, Eileen was free to expand her horizons. She made several audio cassette tapes based on the themes which became her central focus: meditation, faith and prayer, the challenge of change and unconditional love. The tapes led to her giving week-long residential workshops for guests, and to doing more books, including the perennial diary of guidance, *Opening Doors Within,* and her autobiography, *Flight Into Freedom.*

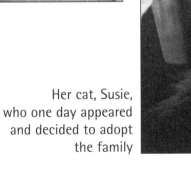

Her cat, Susie, who one day appeared and decided to adopt the family

❧ *Joy* ❧

The fruit of the spirit is joy, so let there be more joy in your life, more fun and laughter.
It is so important that there is balance in all things so life can be enjoyed to the full,
for when there is joy and happiness, you are aware of Me and My divine presence.

❧

You find true joy and happiness in life when you give and give and go on giving,
and never count the cost.

❧

Blessed is that person who brings joy to those souls
who are burdened and lack sparkle in life.
Cast all your burdens upon Me, and bring joy and freedom to all those souls you contact.
Be joy and inspiration, and reflect Me in all that you do, say and think.
Be at perfect peace as you do My will and walk in My ways, glorifying Me.

❧

Live one day at a time. Do not try and rush ahead, making arrangements for tomorrow,
for tomorrow may never come. Enjoy today to the full; enjoy it as if it were your last.
Do all the wonderful things you have longed to do, not recklessly or thoughtlessly,
but with real joy.

With David Earl Platts giving one of their *Learning To Love* workshops for guests in the Beech Tree Room at Cluny Hill College

Her first week-long workshop for guests, *Loving Unconditionally,* 1985

LOVING UNCONDITIONALLY

For some time now, I have felt the primary lesson to learn in life is to love. It has been my experience we have basically only two choices in how we love: we can love conditionally or unconditionally.

A few years ago I was sitting on a bus when I found myself having an inner dialogue with myself. I felt I needed to write it down, so I found an envelope and a pencil in my handbag, and wrote:

> *Can you say to me and I say to you, 'I love you' without either of us feeling uncomfortable, threatened or that something is expected of either of us? Can we love each other, regardless of our age, sex or origin with pure, understanding love? With unconditional love? The world needs this sort of love. All humanity needs this sort of love. Can we love this way? I feel we can, but it is not something simply to be talked about. It is something to be acted upon, to be experimented with.*

That dialogue was the start of a quest for wholeness in my life, and I am still learning how to put this unconditional love into practice. I have read about it, and I have received inspiration in meditation on the subject. I have come to learn unconditional love is an expression of the divinity within each one of us. It is an all-embracing love. It gives acceptance, if not always approval, to everyone and everything. It is unique and universal, within reach of all of us. It is vitalising. It is nurturing. It expects or demands absolutely nothing in return. It is its own reason for being.

I feel we all have a tremendous job to do. It is the silent work of creating more and more unconditional love in the world. It is like the yeast in a lump of bread dough which does its work very quietly and silently without any fuss. Yet without it the bread would be a solid lump. As we begin to love unconditionally, so will the heaviness in our own life be lightened.

I have learned that if we love solely from the emotional level, then we consciously or unconsciously are expecting something in return. Our love is then conditional, and is often possessive, indulgent, needy or sentimental. As long as we function principally from the emotional level, we are a slave to our own emotions, a puppet on the strings of our own emotions, in one emotional melodrama or soap opera after another.

When we function from the level of unconditional love, recognising and giving thanks to the divinity within as the source of this divine love, we begin to know the meaning of freedom, and we are no longer tied up in knots emotionally.

How few of us function from this level! When we do, how often we are misunderstood by those people who function principally from the emotional level! How complicated relationships become when they can be so simple and straightforward! All the more reason for us to change our outlook, our whole way of thinking, if necessary, and so help those around us to change their way of thinking.

I have learned that unconditional love does not come all at once. It starts in small ways and then grows one step at a time. Its benefits are enormous.

Life is more abundant and fulfilling when we choose unconditional love as the primary principle which guides us. It is a deliberate choice we can make, one which serves us, everyone around us and the very planet itself. We transform the world as we transform ourselves with the power of unconditional love.

SNAPSHOTS FROM ON TOUR

Peter and Eileen began to receive invitations from around the world to present talks and workshops based on their pioneering experiences of cooperating with spiritual forces behind nature in the garden and of starting an intentional community based on nondenominational spiritual principles and practices. Tours were organised and in the next few years they visited many western European countries as well as most English-speaking countries in the world. Their presentations attracted more visitors to the Foundation, many returning later to live there. The Foundation soon became an international centre, with more than two dozen countries represented at any given time.

At a talk in Stockholm

In Sweden giving talks and workshops when her book,
The Living Word, was first published in Swedish

❧ *Needs* ❧

If there is a need, know that need is already being met.
It is a case of learning that I already know all of your needs,
and that I meet these needs. But you, with your firm belief, have to manifest them.

❧

Expect only the very best, and expect every need to be met, even the most seemingly
impossible. Never at any time limit yourself or feel that you should not expect too much.
See your needs very clearly, voice them and then have complete faith and confidence
that they will be met.

❧

I know all your needs and will meet them even before you are aware of them yourself,
when you surrender all to Me and leave all in My hands.

❧

You came into this world with nothing, and you will go out of it with nothing.
All you have I have given to you to use to the full while you are on this earth plane.
Why not enjoy everything and give thanks for it all, but do not try to hold on to it.
Freely has it been given to you; freely give it to those souls around you.
Share all you have, and so make room for more and more to be drawn to you.
Know that your every need is wonderfully met as you live by My laws.

At a talk
in Paris

After a
workshop
in Brussels

❧ *Times of Stillness* ❧

Millions of souls in the world cannot bear silence; they have to have
constant noise and action around them. They are restless within and without.
I tell you, times of peace and stillness are very precious in a world of turmoil.
Seek them, find them and remain in them.

❧

To meditate is to know the power of stillness. In many ways nature reveals
the power of stillness: the blooming of a flower is a quiet process.
The miracle of dawn and the glorious sunrise are not heralded with any noise.
The moon and stars appear without fanfare.
All creation is sustained by silent, imperceptible, unfailing law.
Be still, and know that the 'I am' within you is God.

❧

The time you spend in peace and stillness is never wasted.
It is necessary for every soul to find time to be still and reflect on that which is deep within,
on the things that matter in life, that make your life what it is, the ways of the spirit.
It matters not how busy your day may be. Those times of stillness are essential.

In California

By a lake
in Nevada

With Peter and
their hostess in
New Mexico

In New Zealand
at the Nambassa
Festival to give an
illustrated talk

Expectancy

As you expect the very best in life, you draw it to you; so start right now
expecting the very best in everything and everyone, and watch the very best come about.
Expect your every need to be met. Expect the answer to every problem.
Expect abundance on every level. Expect to grow spiritually.
Accept no limitations in your life; simply know and accept that all My good and perfect
gifts are yours as you learn to get your values right and put first things first in your life.
Expect to grow in stature and beauty, in wisdom and understanding.
Expect to be used as a channel for My divine love and light to flow in and through.
Accept that I can use you for My work. Do it all in absolute faith and confidence,
and behold My wonders and glories come about, not just once in a while, but all the time,
so that your whole life is indeed a song of joy and thanksgiving.

My ways are not man's ways, therefore expect the unexpected; be surprised at nothing.

Why not be an optimist in this life, always expecting the best,
always finding the best, always creating the best!
Optimism leads to power; pessimism leads to weakness and defeat.

Taking time out
to relax while
on tour in
South Africa

❧ Attunement ❧

Start the day by getting into tune with Me, by being still
and finding that inner peace and serenity which nothing can destroy.
A sensitive musical instrument has to be tuned before it can be played.
How much more do you have to be tuned each day
before you enter and play your part in the orchestra of life?

To set the pace for the day, you have to learn to attune yourself to a very quiet,
receptive and impressionable state. In that state you will be able to direct the activities
of your mind along the highest and most desirable path.
Enter the new day prepared for the very best to take place in everything you undertake.
Step by step see the perfect pattern unfold for the day and for you.
Yesterday is behind you, a new and glorious day is before you,
and you are in harmony with all life.

When you are in tune with life you will find yourself doing everything at the right time.
All you have to do to get into tune is take time to go into the silence
to find your direct contact with Me.
This is why those times of peace and stillness are so vitally important for you,
far more important than you realise.

With Amanda Haworth
on tour in Brazil

Eileen was a featured
speaker at the
International Peace
Conference in India

THE UNIVERSAL HALL

A major achievement was the design and construction of the Universal Hall, encompassing an auditorium, audio and dance studios, photographic dark room and cafe. It took several years to build, and almost all of the work was done by unpaid volunteers, most of whom had little construction experience.

For 26 years Peter and Eileen worked as two halves of a whole, giving themselves completely to their family and to the Foundation. However the time came for each of them to focus on becoming more independent and whole. They eventually separated, with Eileen choosing to remain in the community and Peter leaving in 1979.

The caravan park with the Universal Hall under construction in the foreground

The Universal Hall

Interior of the
auditorium

❧ Miracles ❧

Expect a miracle.
Expect miracle upon miracle to come about, and do not limit in any way.
The more open you are, the better, for then there is nothing in the way
to stop the flow of My laws, for miracles are simply My laws in action.
Flow with these laws, and anything can happen.

❧

Seek and find your direct link with Me, and retain that link
no matter what is going on around you. That link with Me, the divine,
is the source of all power, and it is this power which creates miracles.
Work with those laws and anything can happen. It is identifying yourself
with the oneness of all life, with all wisdom and all power,
which opens doors and enables the laws to operate within you.

❧

Without awareness you can miss so much which is right there in front of you,
or even within you. Many souls go through life blind to the wonders all around them,
blind to the miracles of nature, and so miss the miracles of life.
Simply going along in the same old way day in and day out will get you nowhere,
and you cannot hope to grow spiritually. You have to want to move forward,
and when you make your own decision to do so, then you will receive help from every side.
The first move is always yours. So do not waste time hanging back,
but take the first step forward and behold miracle upon miracle taking place in your life.

Focalising a community meeting in the Hall with Alex Walker and Mary Inglis

In a skit with Alexis Maxey during a Friday night 'Sharing'

Change

Change is the key that will open all doors for you, change of heart and mind.
When your security is in Me, you will not fear changes, no matter how drastic they may
appear to be. Simply know that every change which takes place is for the very best and for the
good of the whole, whether they are personal changes, changes in the country or in the world.

***

There is a right time for everything. You can try to prevent changes taking place
because you feel safe and secure where you are and would rather stay in the confines
of that which you know rather than move out into the unknown; but in those confines
you will suffocate and die. Try to understand and accept the need to change
with everything that is taking place at this time.

***

Every soul can find direct contact with Me. Every soul can walk and talk with Me if you
want to and accept the fact. You must believe it is possible and you must want to do it;
then you most certainly will. It need not take lifetimes. It need not take any time.
You can change in the twinkling of an eye if you choose to do so.

***

You cannot fill up a full bucket; you have to empty it first. You cannot move
right into the new when you are still clogged up with the old and refuse to let go.
So change and change quickly, for I have need of you.

Popping out of a cake during festivities in the Hall celebrating the community's birthday

Taking part in the Game of Transformation

Clockwise from top: With Patch Adams, founder of the Gesundheit Institute and hero of the eponymous movie;
With Willis Harman, Institute of Noetic Sciences; Bernhard Wosien, who introduced 'Sacred Dance' to the Foundation

⊰≫ Fountain of Youth ≫⊱

Raise your consciousness and realise that you are ageless. You are as young as time,
as old as eternity. As you live fully and gloriously in the ever present now,
you are always as young as the present. You are constantly being reborn in spirit and in
truth. You cannot remain static in this spiritual life. There is always something new and
exciting to learn and to do. Living in a state of expectancy keeps you ever alert and young.
It is when the mind becomes old and dull that life loses all its sparkle and zest.
Keep your mind alert and you can never grow old. The fountain of youth
is in your consciousness. The joy of living is the elixir of life.

When you keep your mind young, fresh and alert, there is no such thing as growing old.
When you have many interests in life and when you enjoy life to the full,
how can you ever grow old? Human beings limit themselves
when they think of three score years and ten as being the fullness of life.
It can be just the beginning for many souls when they awake to the wonder of life,
and in awakening, begin to enjoy it.

With Sir George Trevelyan, former trustee and longstanding friend

Enjoying tea in the sun with Dorothy Maclean at the cafe

With François Duquesne who took over as Foundation Focaliser when Peter left the community in 1979

WHO AM I?

Who am I? What am I doing? Where am I going? Many of us ask ourselves these questions from time to time. I know I have.

Once in meditation when I asked the question, 'Who am I?' I was told to use an affirmation. At the time I did not like the idea of an affirmation, as I felt it was brainwashing, so I put the guidance aside. But every time I meditated on this question, I was given the same answer.

Eventually I asked which affirmation to use and I was given this one, 'I am a beautiful Christ-filled being'. I was shocked! How could I go around saying such a thing! I wouldn't dare. People would think I was going 'round the bend'.

But the inner prompting was so insistent that, in the end, I decided I would try it when I was alone and no one could hear me. So at first I started to mumble halfheartedly, 'I am a beautiful Christ-filled being'. But as I kept on using this affirmation over a period of time, I began to see what was happening, and what it means to use an affirmation.

To begin with, all that was coming from me was just words, empty words which did not mean anything to me. However, as I continued using this affirmation, the words seemed slowly to become alive. Then later I realised that I was becoming the words. Eventually I came to know and accept that I am indeed a beautiful Christ-filled being.

In fact we all are beautiful Christ-filled beings, but we each need to recognise it and accept it. Now I can make this statement without any hesitation because I know it is the truth. I also know from this experience that affirmations used properly are very powerful tools.

Then I asked myself the question in meditation, 'What am I doing on this planet at this time?' The answer I received from within was, 'To serve God and humanity'. As I meditated upon this response, I realised that to serve God is to see God's hand in everything, and to give God the honour and glory for it at all times.

I felt I understood the first part, but I wondered about serving humanity. The inner prompting I received was that the greatest gift I can give people is to turn them within to find the God within themselves so that they can live, move and have their being from their own divine centre.

That is what I always try to do now in my lectures, workshops, books and tapes – direct people to explore more deeply inside themselves until they come to the very core of their being, to their own divinity within.

I feel that it is important for each of us to take time to go into the stillness to find answers to these questions and to the other doubts, fears and inner conflicts we may have about ourselves. I am sure the answers which come to everyone are all different. It doesn't matter. What matters is putting into practice whatever prompting is received in the stillness.

CORNERSTONE

Throughout her life, Eileen had had her own house only once, with Andrew in Surrey. When she left in 1953, she was not to have a house of her own again for 37 years. And then,

I was told from within that I was to have a small house built. I could not imagine how it was going to be done. Where was the money, and where were the hands to build it? In faith, I simply had to hold the vision of this house in my consciousness, and never let it go. Then when I mentioned it to my son who is a builder living in the USA, he said he would be willing to give two months of his time to come to Scotland and put my house up for me. What a wonderful start! Then an architect said he would do the design as a gift. Step by step, I watched the whole plan unfold. It is so uplifting to watch a vision on the inner levels coming into outer manifestation! It is the way the whole of the Findhorn Foundation was brought about over many years.

Designed by London architect Ekkehard Weisner and built by her son, David, with community help, her new house 'Cornerstone' was dedicated in 1990.

Giving a guest a tour of the house while it was being built

The front of Eileen's house with the pink double cherry tree 'Lady Mayo' around which the house was built

Another view facing the Park Community Centre

≪≫ *A*ᴸ

I am the source of all things. I
Think abundance; think prosperity.
When you think limitation, you create lir
you will find that you have dammed up t
Next time you find yourself suffering lac.
your conditions or your situ
and see what there is in you which is caus
short of something? Fear can caus
Cast all your fears and worries upon Me
power and strength, with faith and belie
you will find that the rest of your li

ıdant supply.
k lack or poverty.
u. Before you know it,
ss supply of all things.
ıe your circumstances,
k within
ʼr of lack, fear of being
anything else.
ʼet Me infil you with
ritual values right,
ıe perfection.

≪≫

Why not start right now thinking abundanc

virtue in being poor.

≪≫

Hold the vision of My limitless love evei
of My wonders and glories coming ab
and new earth, of My will being do
and goodwill t
Hold the vision of vast cities of ligf
where peace and loi

ʾss abundance,
ʼ new heaven
ʼ on earth

ʼe world

Holding up a book of photographs showing the stage-by-stage construction, during the blessing of the house

⚘ *Spiritual Life* ⚘

Be not concerned if your beginnings into this spiritual life are small. All good things
have small beginnings. The mighty oak starts from a tiny acorn. From a tiny seed
the most wonderful plants and flowers spring forth. From a tiny seed of love
many lives can be changed.

⚘

There is no mass production in the spiritual life. Each soul has a very special place.
Each soul has a very special destiny. Some need help to realise their destiny.
Others will plod along and reach there in the end. There is no set pattern to follow.
Each one is an individual and should be treated as an individual.

⚘

To live a spiritual life does not mean you are deprived of all those worldly goods
you have need of and that make life easier.
It simply means that you have the use of every single thing you need
to use for the benefit of the whole and to My honour and glory.
When you have finished with it, whatever it may be, it is returned to Me with love
and gratitude, because you recognise that all you have is Mine.

⚘

Everything and everyone responds to love, for love draws the very best out of all,
and where love is, there My spirit is; and where My spirit is,
there is the source of your spiritual life. Seek always that which is deep within you,
and waste no more time seeking for the answer to life from without.

Trying out the bed in her new house

Crystal stealing a cat nap

BEST FRIENDS

Joan Hartnell-Beavis was Eileen's closest friend for many years. She arrived in 1968 and lived in a bungalow across from the Community Centre. She was a very private person, so she said she would try living with the group for a year, and she stayed until her death in 1996. Joanie served as the Foundation treasurer, entertained VIPs at tea, helped in the kitchen, chauffeured Eileen around Morayshire on errands and conscientiously did whatever was needed. Later, when the community was well established, Eileen and Joanie took occasional holidays abroad together, most often to where it was warm and sunny.

As Joanie became more frail, Eileen looked after her. When Joanie had to go to hospital, she was put in a ward with eight other people. Realising Joanie was very unhappy, Eileen decided with the full support of the community to bring her home. Joanie was dying, and Eileen felt she needed to die at home with her own things around her. A principal 'carer' was found and two dozen others in the community volunteered to help. It was the very first time a terminally ill resident was cared for at home, an amazing experience for everyone.

❧❧ Security ❧❧

Where is your security? Is it in people? In your bank account?
Or is it firmly rooted and grounded in Me, the divinity within you?

❧

Let your security be in Me, and in no other. Then you can stand alone and do all things,
for all outer props have been removed, and you find that you can walk in the light
without trying to clutch on to second-hand truths, information or instructions.
Everything comes from deep within you, from the source of all, from Me.

❧

You cannot see what the future holds for you. It does not matter one iota.
All it would do if you could see into the future would be to give you a sense of security.
Your security is in Me, and the only thing that matters is to do My will.

❧

Be like an anchor, strong and steady, so that no storm without can affect you
or shift you from your rightful place. Hold fast and know that all is very, very well,
and that all is proceeding according to My perfect plan.
Let not your heart be troubled, but put your whole trust, faith and security in Me.

Going over to Joanie's bungalow to return her
pension book

❧ *Service* ❧

*When you stop thinking of the self and start thinking of those around you
and how you can help and serve your fellow man, great changes will take place in your life.*

❧

*See that everything you do is dedicated to Me, and is of benefit to the whole.
When you live for the whole, the self is forgotten in service to your fellow man;
and when you are serving your fellow man you are serving Me.*

❧

*Service is a wonderful healer, for as you forget yourself in service,
you will find you will grow and expand in the most wonderful way.
You will reach great heights and plumb great depths,
and your love and understanding of life will begin to mean something to you.*

❧

*Whenever you find yourself with a feeling of discontent and dissatisfaction in life,
you may be sure it is because you have stopped thinking of others and have become
too wrapped up in yourself. The way to change is to start thinking of someone else
and do something for them so that the self is completely forgotten. There are
so many souls in need that there is always something you can do for someone else.*

Taking turns
on the back of
David's motorbike
outside Drumduan

Cooking omelettes
in the Community
Centre kitchen,
with Joanie
serving through
the hatch to a
queue of hungry
people

COMMUNITY CELEBRATIONS

As far as the community is concerned, it is God's community. The spiritual roots have gone deep, deep down – nothing is going to shake them. I was told in meditation, "The leaves may change with the seasons, the branches may be broken off with the winds of change and the storms of confusion, but the trunk is absolutely solid and steady, and the roots are very firmly established so that nothing can uproot them. They are there for all time". That is because this community is rooted and grounded in God; otherwise it would have crumbled a long time ago.

Receiving flowers and appreciations at the community's 25th birthday celebration

Cutting the cake for the community's 30th birthday, November 17, 1992, with Dorothy, Peter, François Duquesne and others

Surrounded by friends during the 30th birthday celebrations

Peace

You contain all within you. You contain within you peace which passes all understanding
and reflect that peace in your outer living and circumstances;
or you contain turmoil within and reflect that without.
You cannot hide that which is going on within, for sooner or later it will be reflected
on the outer. All that you are, all that you do, all that you say stems from within.
Get straight within and you will be straight without, and will be able
to do all that has to be done with a great sense of peace and tranquillity.

Get into tune with Me in the peace and stillness. How can you expect to hear
My still small voice when you are too busy to take time to be still and listen?
As you learn to be still you will be able to do it, no matter what you are doing,
no matter where you are. You will be able to pull your cloak of peace and stillness
around you, and find that centre of peace that nothing can disturb.

Peace starts within. It is there within every soul,
like a tiny seed waiting to germinate and grow and flourish.

Only when you realise fully that you are in the right place at the right time,
doing the work I have chosen for you to do, will you find complete peace
of heart and mind. It is what I want you to do, and find that peace.

Admiring her
birthday cake

FROM THE FAMILY ALBUM

Mother, grandmother, great-grandmother, Eileen has always been grateful for the blessings of her family. While it took time and patience, she made peace with Andrew and her children from the first marriage. From Scotland, England, Canada and New Zealand all eight children came together for the first time in 1997 to celebrate her 80th birthday.

Her first family, Christmas, 1963

⚒ Universal Love ⚒

Hold the vision of perfection, harmony and beauty ever before you,
and see it in everything and everyone. Let the love within you bubble over like water
and flow to all alike. Let there be no discrimination in you, for all are of Me;
all are one family. Universal love starts within each individual and works its way out.
When each individual realises it and allows that love to flow freely, great changes will come
about in the world, for it is love that transmutes all hatred, jealousy, envy, criticism and
greed. These are the qualities that cause war, destruction and death.
Love creates life, life everlasting, life abundant. Love brings with it peace, joy,
and true and lasting happiness and contentment. Above all, it brings unity and oneness.
So if you have wandered off into the highways and byways and lost your way,
come back to the path of love which leads straight to Me,
and there you will find Me waiting deep within you.

⚒

Life without love is like a desert without water, dry, parched, incapable of bringing forth
a living thing. Therefore keep your heart open and the love flowing,
no matter what is happening around you.
Live a vital living life bringing forth life and more life.

⚒

Infinite life cannot be constrained within a narrow concept. Infinite love cannot be confined
in one relationship. Open your heart wide and love all mankind, all creation.

With grandson, Andrew, when visiting her family in Portugal

With grandsons, Clive and Gavin, in New Zealand

❦ Faith ❦

*The universe is in My hands and no one can harm it. Go forward in complete faith
and confidence, allowing My wonders and glories to unfold. Be afraid of nothing,
but be strong and of good courage. When you are at perfect peace within,
you will be able to withstand the stresses and strains without.
Therefore let My peace and love infil and enfold you,
and be at perfect peace as you do My will.*

*You have to have faith in your ability to swim before you jump into deep water
with complete confidence; otherwise you will drown. You have to have faith
in the ability to live by faith before you can do it. Faith begets faith.
How can you tell whether you can trust Me unless you try it and see if it is so?*

*When a small child starts to walk it takes a few faltering steps until it gains confidence.
As it does so, its steps become firmer and surer until eventually it can walk
without stumbling. Then it learns to run and jump, but one stage has to be reached
at a time. So with faith. It has to be built up gradually. It does not come all at once.*

*Now is the time to live by faith, not tomorrow or one day when you are feeling stronger
and have more confidence. Put it into practice right now and see how wonderfully it works.*

With her eldest son, Richard, and two of his children, Patricia and Steven

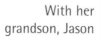

With her grandson, Jason

❧❧ We Are One ❧❧

You are the point of light within My mind. You are the point of love within My heart.
When you can accept it, when you can see yourself as the microcosm of the macrocosm,
you will never again belittle yourself or think ill of yourself.
You will realise that you are indeed made in My image and likeness, that we are one,
and that nothing and no one can separate us. If you feel any separation from Me,
it is of your own making, for I never separate Myself from you.
You are individually what I am universally. Is it any wonder you have to be born again
to accept the wonder of this truth!
So many souls have strayed so far from Me, and have separated themselves to such an
extent that they have placed Me in the heavens at such heights that I am unapproachable.
I am within you, hidden in the very depths, waiting to be recognised and drawn forth.

I want you to know and feel My oneness with you as you have never done before.
Keep affirming 'we are one' until it becomes a part of you.
I am perfect, and as we are one, you are perfect. Have no doubt about it.
I am love. We are one, therefore you are love. I am truth. Therefore you are truth.
I am power. You are power.
Let your soul sink right into this truth that we are one.
Repeat it until you know it with your whole heart, until nothing can make you doubt it.
This deep knowledge that you are no longer apart from Me,
but you are a part of Me, will enable you to do anything.

Jonathan showing
Eileen how to use
the camera

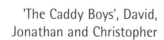

'The Caddy Boys', David,
Jonathan and Christopher

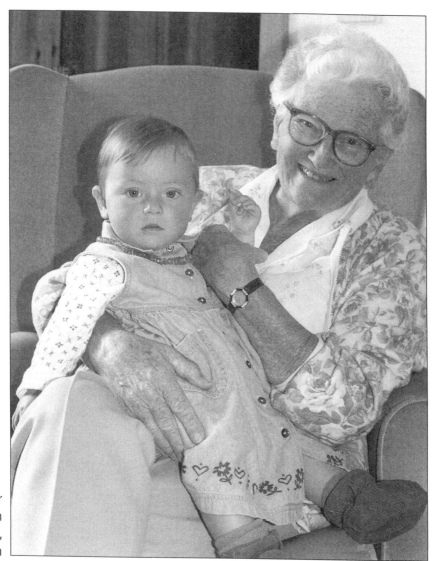

Holding her
19th
grandchild,
Caitlin

Daughter Mary Elizabeth and her two sons came from New Zealand to celebrate Eileen's 80th birthday

The 'Caddy Clan' gathered for her 80th birthday

THE CHALLENGE OF CHANGE

When I see the changes which have taken place in my life and the valuable lessons I have learned and how I have expanded in my outlook, I realise that benefits have come from everything that has happened to me. I have not always seen them at the time.

Like when my father died when I was sixteen, and then my mother only two years later. What good could possibly come from the death of my parents, whom I simply adored? Good did come out of it. How? We had spent a family holiday together, and I had said goodbye to my father before I left to return to boarding school. He was extremely well and full of life. That is the picture I shall always have of him, so I have never been able to see him as being dead. Always I have the feeling that we will meet again and have a wonderful time next holidays.

When my mother died it was different because I was taking care of her at the time. After she passed on, I looked at her and saw only an empty shell. I could feel deep within me that she had shed her old cloak, her body, and had moved into light, and was full of joy to be with my father again. How grateful I am for that very deep experience! It was a real gift to me, for ever since then all that death means to me is moving into the realm of pure spirit which is infinite and eternal. It is returning to the source of all creation.

Another big change came when I married at twenty-one and had five children. My husband was in the Royal Air Force, and we moved every three years. It meant regular change, constant upheaval, adjusting to new countries, new situations, new people. What did it teach me? What was the gift in all this change? To be flexible, knowing change can come in the twinkling of an eye.

After fourteen years of marriage, my husband and I divorced, and I remarried and had three more children. When they all grew up and went off to university, I no longer had the children to look after for the first time in many years. Then when my second husband left, it seemed

I was no longer needed by anyone, and I felt so alone. I had been a mother and housewife for over forty years, and the very idea of coming out of that pattern terrified me. I had felt as safe and secure as a caterpillar in my little chrysalis. But I was stuck in a rut, and I might have remained there, if something in me had not begun to stir.

The wonderful gift of this particular change is that I became more independent, as once I started to move out of my old pattern, I found myself doing things I never thought I was capable of doing: I began talking to large groups of people, giving workshops, travelling all over the world on my own.

I had to do my own thinking, and stand on my own two feet, not in Peter's shadow any longer. I had lost my identity, and I had to find my true self. It was a tremendous struggle. I would not have survived without prayer and meditation; they were my salvation. I am still growing towards a sense of wholeness within myself. I am not self-sufficient, but I am God-sufficient.

I have come to realise there is no going back into my chrysalis. I have had to move forward, to grow, expand and change. That is what makes it so exciting, so rewarding, because there is always something new around the corner; there is always another rung of the ladder to be climbed. So I cease worrying about tomorrow and know that today is all that matters, what I do right now in this moment of time.

Eileen Caddy has touched the lives of thousands of people all over the world. This tribute celebrates her and her divinely ordinary, divinely human service to God and humanity.

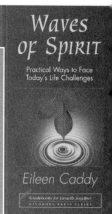

Eileen Caddy's bestselling books and audio-tapes (listed on page 2 of this book)
are available from all good bookstores worldwide,
or directly from publisher Findhorn Press. Order online at findhornpress.com —
or call (850) 893 2920 if you live in the USA or Canada,
or (01309) 690582 if you live in the UK, or +44 1309 690582 if you live elsewhere.